# PIVOT YOUR PERSPECTIVE

Jessica –

# PIVOT YOUR PERSPECTIVE

## YOUR CHANGE JOURNEY

Thank you for all the friendships & love. Glad you are on my Journey!

**JOHN H. SPENKER**

Love, J

**PEACH ELEPHANT** PRESS

Pivot Your Perspective: Your Change Journey is designed to provide information that the author believes to be accurate on the subject matter it covers, and is written from the author's personal experience. In the text that follows, many people's and company's names and identifying characteristics have been changed, so far that any resemblance to actual persons, living or dead, events, companies or locales is entirely coincidental.



First Printing, 2017

Peach Elephant Press
createnonfiction.com

# Acknowledgements

Thank you to my husband, Robert, for the tireless support and endless hours helping me sort and edit my thoughts on paper. I could not have done it without you.

Thank you to my friends who provide encouragement and support when I need it most. Thank you for making the journey so much fun.

Thank you to each of my clients who have helped me translate what I think, feel, and know about personal development into real world application. You inspire me to keep doing what I am doing.

# CONTENTS

# INTRODUCTION

I remember like it was yesterday, sitting in my bedroom crying; sobbing, rocking back and forth while I tried hopelessly to soothe myself. My eyes frantically scanned the room, searching for something comforting to fixate upon: the bunk bed I was sitting on, the pirate curtains lazily flapping in the breeze which my grandmother made, the fresh color of the green walls. I tried desperately to make sense of the craziness of my circumstances. I tried to sort it all out, to figure out how to better plan or be prepared. I felt so alone. I remember those tears, and again, for the third time that day, I made sure my room was as neat and orderly as it could be, as it *had* to be.

I was five, and I know now that those early years could have happened no other way. In the usual brilliance of hindsight, I realize it was an intensive boot camp providing me with real-time, first-hand experience of how to get comfortable with chaos and uncertainty. I learned to dig deep and better understand who I was, and leverage that understanding as the basis from which to experience the world. I learned to move past the circumstances to gain a perspective of what they had to offer—hidden in these circumstances were many gifts.

One gift was a new outlook and fresh perspective on my relationship with change. Fundamentally, change is moving from a current state to a future state, where the middle is transition—seems pretty straightforward. What excites me is looking beneath the current and future "states of being" to see the energy, inertia, and propulsion behind the change. Yes, it is still about the literalness of going from old to new—but now it is also about movement and energy, and how I can make a choice regarding this energy. Am I saying yes or no to the energy of change? Am I aware that this energy aspect is related, but somewhat different, to the literal change itself?

The world around us naturally and continuously evolves and changes. How you and I choose to operate within this continuous field of change becomes a critical area to consider and understand.

Change means different things to different people. At the polar extremes, there are those who function well with change and those who do not, and in the middle of the spectrum lie varying degrees of experience with a broad range of trade-offs. For those who desire to neutralize change so that they can experience more consistency, there lies a conundrum. How do you operate in a world of natural, evolving change, when you are most happy —most grounded — in consistency? It becomes rather exhausting. To further complicate matters, how do you find consistency when the change not only includes elements of day-to-day life, but also dips deeply into core belief systems and psychosocial frameworks?

The spectrum of changes we face varies. Maybe you want to change your career, or maybe you were just fired and somebody changed it for you. Perhaps you have decided to end a long-term relationship, or perhaps a family member has unexpectedly passed on. What's fascinating about change is that no matter how severe or slight, the core remains the same. You have made a choice or you have been dealt a card, but either way, you'll need to find your way through it.

We all have perspectives that are as unique as our personalities; therefore, how we each deal with change will be unique as well. Mine is specific and tailored to my life experiences and circumstances. Yours is distinct and perfect for your life experiences and circumstances. At the end of the day, the common factor is the fact that each one of us is constantly in the midst of transformative change—whether severe or slight. Are you equipped to deal with it? As I reflect, I was never "officially" trained or equipped to deal with change, but I know with confidence that the fundamental conditions of my early years created circumstances and events by which I was both pushed and inspired to find my way through to new understandings and pivots in perspective. Over the years, I have observed the same phenomenon with my clients. Thus, part of our conversation targets the issues at hand and another part focuses in on the mechanics of change; what they were taught or not taught, what is assumed, and how to create new understandings of change mechanics.

## A NEED FOR CONTROL

As a young child, I developed a need for consistency very early on. I struggled with the lack of emotional availability of two parents, who in turn struggled with their emotional readiness. What I know now is that their struggle and mine set in motion the perfect situation for the learning that would change my life and help me help others.

The emotional availability—or lack thereof—of my parents had a profound impact on my parental connection and nurturing. I grew up wanting to make deep emotional connections, and having my core family unable to do so created a situation that was "charged" with kinetic energy. I struggled both with my family and with my close friends as I projected my experience outward in a desperate attempt to resolve it.

The emotional instability of the family situation, mixed with the emotional unavailability, worked to intensify and polarize the experience for me. My experience varied from structure to free-fall to chaos.

**EMOTIONS HELP TO FACILITATE OUR JOURNEY JUST LIKE A COMPASS CAN HELP YOU DETERMINE WHAT DIRECTION TO TAKE AS YOU REVIEW A MAP.**

I began to recede more and more into myself, retreating from the world and building my psychological walls of protection.

Uncertain about the specifics of our life experiences, we all quite normally seek methods to soothe ourselves and to make sense of our surroundings—so that we can be and feel safe. My experience drove me to make a pact with myself—I vowed to always try to figure things out, no matter how much "life" confused me. I vowed to work my way forward. I promised to take the feeling of helplessness and use it to propel myself forward—to transcend that feeling to one where I was in control. It was a life-changing moment that I did not realize was pivotal until my early thirties. It became so much a part of who I was, so core to how I operated in this world, that it was both seen and unseen. It was omnipresent. At the time of the pact, I was little, maybe five or six, so my sphere of control was limited. But I owned those things I could, in fact, control. I will clean my room. Iwill go to school. I will get good grades. I will figure this out, because I know there's a way. I know now that I wanted to push the feeling of desperation far away into a corner. Later, my healing came from going into the corner, sitting with the desperation, and getting to know it from a place of honor—for it served me and was the reason why I was able to learn what I have learned.

Many people consciously or unconsciously choose a behavior to latch onto in these circumstances. I chose to be obsessive and compulsively organized and clean. My room was always perfect. I focused intensely on my grades, always trying to strive for perfection wherever I could. It wasn't that I wanted to be perfect, perfection was just a necessary outcome. You get perfection from doing something else. That something else was my focus—I needed to do the best that I could. I have a phrase that came out of that period: I never leave something worse than I found it.

That motto drove me relentlessly forward in school, and anytime I had troubles, I was deeply distraught. A "C" grade meant something different to me than it would for anybody else—it said I was not going to pull myself out of my chaotic family situation.

It meant there was a flaw in the plan, and my safety was jeopardized.

My plan worked to keep me safe, and I worked intently on my plan. The flaws started to appear in my early twenties. It began with exhaustion. Striving for perfection is a 24-hours-a-day, 7-days-a-week endeavor. It requires a high degree of mental and physical commitment. Around the age of twenty-three, I hit the wall.

What came next was a series of life events that served to break the trance I was in and bring about some interesting pivots. First, circumstance brought me to an excellent therapist. It was the first time I felt heard, and it was the first time I was exposed to tools that enabled me to start adapting and modifying the rigor and strictness of my motto. I began to see myself apart from the circumstances. I had a long way to go, but the idea of the self as core and the environment serving to provide experience was seeded. The idea piqued my curiosity; I wanted to understand more.

Life does not give you more than you can handle. When you are in the middle of it, however, it certainly does not feel that way. As a result, I started to party a little too hard, and that brought about some hard lessons. I know now that those lessons were essential for my learning. I had to hit rock bottom because my promise to work hard and move forward had such a strong hold over me that it had to be crushed or nothing would change. Yet there were still elements of fear within me clutched tightly to retain control over, no matter how much I was learning. As always, the universe brought me a situation that provided the opportunity to learn to let go.

Working myself out of the big hole I had dug for myself, the universe brought an intuitive healer to me. I was a skeptic, and proceeded with caution. My fear of the world falling apart and the feeling of not being safe worked to push me forward. I had nothing else to lose. Desperation can be a friend at times. For 10 years, I worked on and off with this amazing person who, herself, was on her journey to perfect her life's work. I remember the day when she said, "You will do what I do, but differently." I laughed and said, "Yeah, right." Reflecting back on her statement, I know now that I did not believe in myself, and having someone acknowledge what I secretly knew deep down sparked my own natural curiosity. An idea that was buried came to light, setting off close to two decades of work—reading, learning, practicing, doing.

I became intimately familiar with the power of perspectives—yours and mine. While I was deep in my own story in my younger years, my perspective had served to both move me forward and create circumstances for me to learn. At times, the learning left me feeling like I the wind had been knocked out of me. I often ask my clients, "When do you learn more? When you win the lotto or when you go bankrupt?" Instead of being at odds with the events that I deemed negative, what if they were essential for everything I have today that is good and great?

I learned about how to make the vision real, even when I could not see the vision for myself yet! The next step in a journey is not always the right one. It is just a step. We tend to unconsciously project expectations of good or bad on that step. We evaluate the step from the vantage point of, "Did it get me closer to my dream?" or "Was it the most efficient step?" Although the evaluation has meaning and purpose, there is something to be said about the act of just taking the step, about the "unknowingness" of the next step, and the uncertainty of its outcome magically held in balance in the strength of vision and dream.

I discovered that when I operate from curiosity, I have an endless amount of energy, and work does not feel like work anymore. I know we have all heard that before, and we strive for it, but it can sometimes feel like it eludes us. *What if the experience of work as fun is never perfected?* What if we are constantly learning about how to make our work fun? Maybe the work you do today is not as fun as you would hope, but you can start to take a class or pick up a book or start a conversation to ask someone who has knowledge you can leverage. It is the composite of these baby steps that, when looked at in hindsight, clearly highlights the trajectory to success.

## A JOURNEY INTO COACHING

I am proud of the journey I have traveled thus far. The journey led me to answer the call of coaching, and coaching led me to this book. The areas of focus we will be considering have been essential in almost every client conversation I have had to date; they are topics that come up time and time again, all rooted around our ability to embrace change.

My company provides professional coaching, and I focus on individuals who are typically in the vice grip of change—they are literally in the middle. In the public sector, this includes anyone and everyone who feels the squeeze of everyday life. In the corporate sector, this primarily includes mid- to senior-level management, because they most often act as the conduit (shock absorber) between senior management and the broader workforce. They help implement decisions that can be contrary to the needs or wants of the general workforce. Conversely, they attempt to help the workforce be heard. I coach people like you, who open your email in the morning, and sigh as you review your inbox and attempt to reconcile all the things that you feel you have no control over. Whether that is your superior, changes to your insurance, or your company being acquired, or maybe it is a notice from a utility that your bill is late, and you know you paid it. These are the people I work with.

I am brought in under the guise of helping to deliver a project, often as a program or change manager, where the client seeks help to deliver a specific solution or turn around work that has veered off course. Included in that work are both people and process components. We can set up the best systems, but if we do not keep the people and their ability to execute the changing processes, we will fall short of the goal.

## TWO KINDS OF PEOPLE

Readers of this book will fall into one of two categories: either you need more framework (aka process) in your life, or you need less. The people who need more frameworks are typically more artistically inclined; they function predominantly with their right-brain hemisphere. They work from a place of inter-relatedness. For them, frameworks can feel restrictive and present the sensation of pressure. They are formidable because their world is one of free association, intuition, and feeling. However, there needs to be a delicate balance and synergy between the two worlds of left and right brain. Without balance, our performance, cognition, ability to gain new perspectives, and effort extended to obtain our goals will be challenging.

Those who thrive using frameworks, the left-brainers, have many strengths as well; but without balance, they have challenges to overcome. Deeply focused on process, they discount intuition and feelings—which are equally essential to the journey at hand.

There is a skillset that you and I must have so we can operate day to day with balanced right-left brain thinking. It requires us to have diligence and precision of ability with both the right and left brain so we can dance the delicate dance of balance between both.

This is also where the term "agility" comes in. That term can drive me crazy because it is so overused. "I need to be more agile!" What does that even mean? Personally, when I think of "agile," I envision a shock absorber on a car. It contracts and expands in reaction to its environment. If I hit a bump, the shock absorber reacts to keep me steady. If you are going to be "agile," it implies that you must be able to anticipate, react, and stay fortified. This can feel a little onerous. It also means that you must trust the shock absorber to do its job; there is a bit of faith involved. This can feel a little scary. By finding balance between fortifying ourselves and having faith or a sense of knowing, we are prepared for whatever life has in store for us—not an outcome, but instead, part of our continuous learning.

## THE BENEFIT OF BALANCE

Consider the right-brained person. They are strong, they have amazing gifts, they are often astoundingly artistic, but in my experience, these folks often struggle with the process. They typically have a fantastic idea to start a business, for example, but they might struggle with the business process or with finances. Conversely, consider the left-brained person. They too are strong, they have amazing gifts, they are great with logic and analytics—but they struggle with intuition and things that are not part of a hypothesis.

These examples can sound cliché, but the point is, there are archetypes for both right and left-brained people, and we see those archetypes struggle in similar ways. The fact remains that balance between both sides will help you engage with change in incredible ways. The problem is, most people don't know what they don't know. It is difficult to self-diagnose that which you have a hard time observing. If only it were as easy as realizing, "Hey, I'm really relational. I'm really in my right brain. Maybe I need to retool the other side. I'm going to go figure out how to do that!"

But that is not what happens. Usually, people spin; they spin, and they twirl, and they whirl, getting continually more frustrated.

## KNOWING WHERE YOU STAND

The benefit of this book will be self-diagnosis, and knowing how to apply new knowledge of self once you have it. Remember, we don't know what we don't know. Where do you stand on the right or left-brained spectrum? What are your weaknesses? What are your tendencies? More importantly, what changes will happen once you know?

Once you realize you might be operating in a certain way, you are free to have a real perspective shift. You will have more options, and with more options comes more freedom. You won't be stuck spinning indefinitely, because with the knowledge of your blind spots comes the opportunity to learn and create new choices.

Once you understand where you are, you can orient yourself and adjust. For example, once I have a compass, I can figure out whether I am north, south, east or west, and make a better, informed choice on which direction to take. It is when I am drifting, without orientation, that I don't know if I am going left or right, or even whether I am moving forward. That is the moment where we lose valuable time and can experience real frustration, wasted effort, and alienation.

When we listen deeply to ourselves, we can identify if we lack orientation. If we are feeling constriction, dissonance, or loss, like we are wasting our time or not getting where we want to be, that tells us something. Emotions help to facilitate our journey just like a compass can help you determine what direction to take as you review a map. *Feelings provide critical awareness and guide us to act.*

Part of knowing where you are is knowing how you got there. As a people, as a species, as a tribe, we create shared perspectives for each other on various psychosocial concepts and topics. These are embedded within us. Some perspectives are inherited; some are curated. Our view of change is no exception.

Typically, most of us do not like change. It represents uncertainty. It represents pressure or discomfort. This can be partly inherited from your tribe. How does your familial background handle change? As a child, did you sit at the breakfast or dinner table with your mom and dad and talk about your day? How did they mentor change for you, and what tools or strategies did they expose you to?

The minute we can say, "change is good," is when we can start to build a healthy change perspective. Change is fundamental, it is essential. So why are we so determined to fight it?

"I hate change," you might say, but you know what? The truth is, if you're not changing, you're not living.

## TECTONIC SHIFTS

If you shift your perspective of change, you can shift your level of satisfaction, prosperity, and happiness. Politically, it has never been more important than now to be adept, skilled, and comfortable with change. What is extraordinarily clear is that the volume and magnitude of change happening around us is of monumental scale.

If you do not want to embrace change, then this book is not for you right now. You might not be ready. Know that it is okay. This book is not going to be for everyone, or even for everyone right now, but know that this book is here when you are ready. This book is meant to support your change journey, providing you with a new slant on change, thereby capitalizing on perspectives you might not currently allow yourself to have.

This book is about your JOURNEY. Each one of you is on your own unique journey. Each of you has desires and goals, as well as fears and obstacles. Your journey is between what was and what is yet to be. Your journey is one of change.

This book is about your PERSPECTIVES. Change is not a thing that has to be dealt with, but instead is an energy source—the most basic source of momentum we have available to us. When we interact with change, we initiate a journey of movement and momentum. Change is organic, natural, and essential. It is fundamental to who we are and is part of our human nature. Ask yourself, "How much do I love change?"

This book is about YOU. What do you need to know that you have not thought of, that can help you be the best of who you want to be? If there are perspectives that you have not allowed yourself to acquire yet because you don't know what you don't know, how does that impact not only your journey and your learning, but who you ARE in the journey?

As with any journey, there is the first step. Let's get started, shall we?

# CHAPTER 1:
## Our Understanding of Change

Change, in its simplest form, is the act of moving from a current state, through a transitional state, to a future state. Change is the universal process supporting you and me to move from yesterday to today to tomorrow. On the surface it sounds simple; however, it is not easy. It is pervasive, permeates every area of our life, and creates stress for a great majority of us. We are literally *always* in a state of change! Because it's so constant and all-encompassing, we become oblivious to it—much like we forget about breathing or blinking our eyes. It is only when our breathing is labored or our eyes are dry that we begin to take notice. Only when change challenges us and we fight the challenge do we begin to take notice.

As I did in the introduction, I am going to use the concept of left-brain and right-brain throughout our discussion of change. Having a shared language and understanding will be essential from here on out. The left-brain is verbal, logical, structural, and of a sequential-processing orientation- typically, looking at individual pieces first, and then creating a holistic

**CHANGE, IN ITS SIMPLEST FORM, IS THE ACT OF MOVING FROM A CURRENT STATE, THROUGH TO A TRANSITIONAL STATE, TO A FUTURE STATE.**

picture. The right-brain is non-verbal, intuitive, and of a more instinctual, simultaneous-processing orientation- typically, looking at the holistic picture, and then the individual pieces. Neither modality trumps the other; both have shared importance. What is essential to understand is that most of us have a tendency to face change in either a left-brained or a right-brained way.

It can be said that, emotionally, most of us are averse to change. Why is that? It is because change can take a negative form—like losing something or someone we love and enjoy. It triggers an embodied experience for us. We FEEL change, and even if we define it by both negative and positive emotions, the negative experiences create the most emotional aversion to change.

Our emotional embodiment of a change event triggers our right-brain or left-brain tendency. Meaning, if I have a left-brain tendency, then while under emotional duress, I will tend to gravitate towards a left-brain style of response. This in itself is not negative; however, what we forgo is the opportunity to *assess* the change event—to *understand* if the event calls for more process and rigor, or creativity and intuition. A lack of awareness on our part creates a situation where we could apply the wrong approach and *not realize it.*

When you or I initiate change, it is usually after some period of introspection. Even when the change seems quick and radical, when we look back, we can see trail markers that indicate the change was thought about for some period of time before being initiated. What is important to understand is that the change initiator (you or I) has had *time* to ramp up mentally and emotionally, thoroughly processing the change prior to activating it. Conversely, the change receiver or receivers have not had the same opportunity to ramp up. It becomes important, then, to think about the needs of those on the receiving end of the change—particularly their time to prepare, process, and come to terms with the change they are being asked to participate in. Additionally, understanding your right or left-brain tendency is important, because where you are most dominant will determine how you convey the change, and that conveyance might or might not be what is *needed by the receiver.* Know your tendency and know your audience.

**THE TWO STATES, RIGHT OR LEFT-BRAIN, ARE NOT DISTINCT FROM ONE ANOTHER BUT INSTEAD BLEND SEAMLESSLY INTO ONE ANOTHER. THERE IS A NATURAL DANCE BETWEEN THE TWO STATES, AND IF WE EMBRACE THAT PERSPECTIVE, WE UNLOCK OPPORTUNITY, POTENTIAL, AND PURPOSE.**

We each have an individual level of comfort—or discomfort— with change. Knowing where you are on that scale is important. Are you aware of the framework of change? Do you have an understanding of change as a natural process? Are you aware of your emotional reactions or resistance to change? Each and every one of us has a change bias; you either like it or you don't like it. Are you anxious or calm or somewhere in the middle? Know there is a natural point where you and I fight change, and there is a point where you and I become determined to take change head on. Have you ever asked yourself where you are on the change scale? Have you asked if your acceptance or resistance to change differs depending upon circumstance? Are you even aware that there is a change scale?

In addition to our tendencies toward right or left-brained processing, our individual change biases are learned and intensified by the core family, friends, and acquaintances, or what I will term as "tribes," that we surround ourselves with. Our familial heritage provides a core bias regarding change. Our friends and acquaintances, as well as the companies we work with and for, have their own individual change biases from which we learn and, subsequently, incorporate into our individual change bias. What have you inherited from your tribe?

The two states—intuitive versus logical, right versus left-brained—are not distinct from one another. They blend seamlessly into one another. There is a natural dance between the two states, and if we embrace that perspective, we unlock opportunity, potential, and purpose. Looking at change from both a functional state and a feeling state is the key to helping us harness change energy.

## OUR CHOICE, OUR CHANGE

For over 15 years, I lived in Southern California and I absolutely loved it. In my twenties and thirties, I could not have been in a better place. In my late thirties, ready for a change, I decided to move to the Pacific Northwest. Many along my change journey second-guessed me. "Why are you leaving? You have a home and friends! You have a good life, why are you shaking that up? Come on, it's sunny in California! It rains in the Pacific Northwest!" It became a controversial topic—although I would point out the controversy came from love, as everyone wanted the best for me. Fast-forward through many long, wintery, rainy days, and the perspective my tribe had was correct; honestly, I could have disliked the Pacific Northwest. I could have gotten angry at myself, at my decision-making. The weather was bleak enough at times to inspire it. But the truth is, I did not get mad. How could I be angry? I made an informed decision and I knew what I was getting into. There was no room for blame, and besides, what good would that have done? Focusing on blame is not focusing on the issue at hand. Blame is a distraction. Wherever and whenever we can divert our attention from blame to the issue, we increase change efficiency and improve our change experience.

The degree to which you and I can be of conscious choice directly represents the power we have available to us at any one moment. I always knew the Pacific Northwest was going to be rainy, right? And because

I knew, I had power. I had a choice. I understood the trade-offs of the change, and so the change was less stressful for me. Instead of losing time and energy to frustration, I created a different experience for myself. Reflecting back, I had the best seven years of my life.

When working with my clients, I use the concept of arithmetic to help us understand where we are in our

**WE CREATE CHANGE FOR OURSELVES AND WE INTERACT WITH THE CHANGE CREATED BY OTHERS. IF WE CAN BE AWARE OF THIS, INTERALIZE IF, THEN WE CAN START TO UTILIZE CHANGE AS A TOOL.**

decision making process. Are we in front of the problem or behind the problem? Let us take a simple arithmetic equation such as 1+1=2. It is straightforward, right? Now, let us use the same equation to help understand our decision making and how that informs our change experience. To the right of the equal sign is the outcome of our decision. To the left of the equal sign are the *decision* integers that string together to help us reach an outcome.

### DECISION EQUATION: DECISION INTEGER 1 + DECISION INTEGER 2 + DECISION INTEGER 3 = OUTCOME

Looking at my move as an example, if my outcome was blame (right side of the equal sign), then I was most likely angry with one or more of my decisions along the way—the integers—to produce that outcome. For example, I could have been upset that I did not thoroughly research the weather, resulting in my making an uninformed decision. More true for each of us is that cold, hard facts are trumped by idyllic notions. Rather than not doing any research, I could have had read a book or seen a movie that created a vision of what the Pacific Northwest "could be." That type of idyllic notion has the opportunity to overpower facts. Often, we do not realize that until later. When that happens, we experience blame or some other outcome.

Where do you stand in the Decision Equation? Do you operate to the left of the equal sign making decisions, or to the right, stuck in the outcome, without power? When we consciously operate on the left of the equal sign, we have decision integers we can add and subtract, which absolutely impact the outcome. When you operate from the right of the equal sign, we are already experiencing an outcome, and any new decision is now about pivoting an undesirable outcome to something desirable. *Having a perspective that decisions string together to create an experience is a powerful perspective to have.* Understanding the impact of decisions on life experience is not new—I am confident you have heard this before. I am not confident, however, that you have really broken this down, like we have with the equation, so that you grasp the idea that the power you have to influence outcomes is more than you realize.

**MY LIFE AND MY EXPERIENCE IN EACH OF THOSE EMOTIONS ARE VERY DIFFERENT; THE PERSPECTIVE SHIFT COMES WHEN WE REALIZE WE DO NOT HAVE TO ALLOW OUR CIRCUMSTANCES TO DICTATE OUR EMOTIONS. INSTEAD, OUR EMOTIONS INFORM OUR EXPERIENCE.**

If change is a journey from point A to point B, then our power comes in the middle. The transition state between current and future state. What decisions are you making? What steps are you taking? How many transactions are there?

The idea of being at choice—the act of being completely conscious in the moment so as to make an informed choice—becomes fuzzy when life is emotionally charged. It is easy to speak in metaphors and examples and *postulate* that your emotions should not take over, but it is difficult to maintain when we are in the middle of our own tableau. How aware are you of your change triggers? What if you are pushed to do something you historically have not been able to do or do well? You either learn you are good at something you thought you were not, or you reconfirm that the something remains a struggle for you. What if the latter outcome is impacted by a historical perspective of what you don't do well, as well as your bias towards change? Meaning, I have always struggled with a certain skill and I also dislike change. This represents a powerful one-two punch.

Understanding our biases when we are presented with change decisions helps to ensure we are not robbed of an opportunity to make a new choice and, thereby, create new outcomes. What if understanding my ability or inability regarding a skill is based on outdated information? What if my decision is compounded by my natural bias to avert change?

## CHANGE AS POWER

Life changes are the propulsion of our life's journey, and the change framework helps to inform us and help us make informed choices. Life is about constant change, and it is possible to get to a place of embracing change—both positive and negative. Power comes from our ability to navigate—to understand where we are in the journey from today to tomorrow and where we are in our Decision Equation. This represents a giant step, and for most of my clients, it is a huge "a-ha!" moment. When we float around, unsure, unaware of where we are, we decrease our ability to impact our destination and our outcomes. For example, how do you know how to head south on a street if you don't know where you are? Orientation matters. If you don't know your orientation, you will waste energy and effort. That said, it is also true that we need to experience floating around as a state of learning, so we have a visceral understanding of what "not knowing" is. This helps to inform us so that we emotionally and intellectually know what it feels like to be in or out of orientation. Our ability to find our orientation is directly aided by frameworks such as a change or decision frameworks. Have you thought about frameworks in this way before?

Know that the goal is not to remove the experience of pain or fear of the unknown. All experiences provide us with learning. We cannot appreciate the light until we have experienced the dark. The human experience is to learn from contrast, from what you like as well as dislike, from what you love as well as fear. The goal is about becoming aware of where you are (orientation) and preparing yourself for something new or for re-experiencing something you thought you knew or understood, but did not. It is about leveraging tools such as frameworks to improve awareness so you can maximize the power of change.

If you are reading this book, you might be thinking, "I know I need to learn something that I didn't know before." Step one is simply being aware that you are always, every moment, every day, in transition. Today is the transition from yesterday to tomorrow. Transition and change are a way of life. Knowing this, viscerally understanding it, fundamentally changes how we go about our life's journey. Additionally, this understanding impacts the level of ease with which you go about your day.

The concept of change as propulsion energy is an outcome of shifting our understanding of change itself. Change does not happen to us. Instead, we create change for ourselves and we interact with the change created by others. If we can be aware of this, internalize it, then we can start to utilize change as a tool.

## WHY PERSPECTIVE MATTERS

We are grounded by the structure from which we operate—and that structure we create for ourselves.

It is true that we are the receivers of environmental structure as well, but we have a choice to accept or question. If we are operating from the perspective that change is dangerous, stressful, and negative, we create a particular experience. If we work from the point of view that change is a fight or opposition, then we are setting ourselves up for a very specific experience. What if we operate from a lens that change is natural and that we are meant to be within the change framework willingly? That puts a very distinct experience in front of us with an explicit construct, gentler steps, and pleasant places to walk through. What if I operate from a place where change is a tool, a source of energy to get me from today to tomorrow?

I know what it is like to be hateful and angry. I also know what it is like to be loving and happy. My life and my experience in each of those emotions are very different; the perspective shift comes when we realize we do not have to allow our circumstances to dictate our emotions. Instead, our emotions inform our experience. In the same day, we can experience bankruptcy, winning or losing the lotto, buying a house, or getting cancer. How will they affect me? What perspectives do I have available to me in each of these moments? Do I question my perspectives and biases before I blindly embrace them and leverage them?

Limiting perspectives live as our own personal myths. Usually, when we're listening to them, we tend to be individualized and isolated. The isolation disrupts the support of others. Once we can connect to a fresh perspective, we can align to the truth of who we are, and connect to the support systems that are there to help us.

Facing life without observing and taking note of your perspectives is like throwing random ingredients into a cooking pot and hoping spaghetti comes out. You are not really participating. You might get lucky with a good meal every once in a while, but more often, you will end up with something you cannot eat. Are you okay with that? Are you satisfied with taking chances with perspectives you have not explored resulting in experiences you do not want? Or do you want to live intentionally?

The change framework is a tool at your disposal; use it, or be used.

# CHAPTER 2:

## Separating the What and the How

*What* is it that I want to do, and *how* do I get there? It is common to commingle and confound the *what* and the *how* on the change journey. Each has a particular area of focus, and you need both to navigate change successfully. Yet people have trouble distinguishing them, or they over-index on one or the other. It is typical to focus on the *what* over the *how*, or vice versa. Our tendency to rely on one over the other goes back to the left or right-brained orientation.

Right-brained people tend to be conceptualists. They are great at the *what*. They love their ideas and are incredible at generating them. The left-brainers are better at the *how*, implementing to-dos with measurable structure. Mixing the *what* and the *how* can bring frustration and confusion. My clients bring situations forward asking, *"Why isn't this working?!"* When we better understand the situation at hand, it becomes clear they have a predominant focus. They either have a fully fleshed-out idea that is incredible and inspiring, but has limited structure to bring it to fruition, or they have too much structure and the structure impedes the progress of the idea.

If you haven't guessed it, I am usually the latter. Historically, I have over-indexed in the *how*. When I think of great ideas, I quickly move into implementation, focusing more on the process than the idea itself. I am eager to add structure and tactics. My success, however, comes from realizing this and intervening accordingly. Once I am aware of my tendency, I create an opportunity to insert the necessary time to explore the idea and connect to the inspiration.

Our dominance can be situationally based, and as such, we can have a dominant tendency that is scenario or context-based. For example, we can look at my journey to write this book. Surprisingly, I had all the ideas fully fleshed-out, and not once did I experience writer's block. I knew the *what,* but was stuck on the *how*. This contradicted my historical pattern of being stronger in the how. No matter how many times I sat down to write, I would get distracted or frustrated with the writing process. After a few years, I simply gave up. One day, I happened across an email offering a service to those who have ideas but are struggling to bring them to light. At first, I dismissed the email thinking to myself, "I don't need that." I realized, however, that I was saying that because traditionally I am super-successful with the how. Maybe it was time to hand over the how to those that can help. I did! The fact that this book is a reality is because I understood I needed help with the how of writing it, and that maybe I am not as universally good at the how as I thought!

## WHAT THE WHAT?

In the simplest terms, the *what* is the goal, aspiration, or dream. It can be a book, relationship, or career. It can be the aspiration that "I want to make a million dollars," or "I want a big house," or "I want a different lifestyle." The *how* is the process of making the goal or dream a reality. What is the sequence of events needed to accomplish the goal? What are the tradeoffs I am willing to say "yes" and "no" to in order to support the process I need to complete to make the dream come true?

When I committed to writing this book, I was finally saying "yes" to it. I was saying "yes" to the work required to create a book, which also meant I must say "no" to something else—such as billable client time, family time, or carefree weekend time. I made an informed decision based on the tradeoffs of my time so I could create my book. I made an informed choice. There was now no option for me to be upset later because I had less time for family or friends. I was *at choice* with my decision. To demonstrate, let's circle back to the Decision Equation. I am choosing to operate to the left of the equal sign. Working with the Decision Integers, I consciously think through all of the things that I value spending my time on. I chose to increase time on writing, and decrease time on family, friends, and free time. I did so knowing it was not forever, but for a specific period of time. I did so knowing the outcome, the right side of the equal sign, was the book. Acting from an informed state of mind helped me to understand choices, the tradeoff of yeses and noes, so that I can intently impact the desired outcome—this book!

**UNDERSTANDING THE WHAT AND THE HOW STRENGTHS FACILITATES YOUR ABILITY TO GET TO THE ROOT OF PROBLEMATIC SITUATIONS; PARTICULARLY SITUATIONS THAT YOU FIND YOURSELF IN REPEATEDLY.**

By not taking the time to separate and better understand the *what* and the *how* of our goals, we will inherently assume that we have no bias or natural inclination for one over the other. This creates blind spots. The first step here is to ask yourself: do you realize that the two polarities exist? And from there, do you know what your *what* and *how* tendencies are, and if you tend to index in the what over the how or vice versa? Once you understand and acknowledge your tendency, you confirm the awareness of the tendency. Once you have the awareness, you create the opportunity to approach any situation differently, thereby creating opportunity for new outcomes. The perspective that we operate in the *what* and *how* is powerful and provides a tool to support us to be more aware and more in the moment.

## OVERCOMING THE STRUGGLES

Without the *what* and *how* distinction, you increase stress and decrease choice, and success will be limited by your own unnamed tendency to index on one over the other. Separating the what and your how helps to avoid that fateful experience of, "*I'm always doing this, it never works,*" or "*I'm bad at this,*" or "*my ideas are bad.*" These feelings (which are associated with failure), without the knowledge of what is causing them, become false facts, and only set us up for more disappointment.

Understanding your *what* and *how* strengths facilitates your ability to get to the root of problematic situations; particularly situations that you find yourself in repeatedly. What if I said, "*I don't want to write this book because I don't have a great idea*"? Because I have shared with you already that I had no problem with the idea (the *what*), but instead had a problem with writing (the *how*), not understanding the dichotomy of the what and how could have left me with a false fact and, thereby, sent me on a path to find the wrong solution.

Clients work with me because they seek a resolution or a specific outcome. One of my clients had a strong desire to help people through the use of visual arts (such as comics) as a means to help people connect with themselves. It was a dream that felt far away. In his current job as an instructional designer, he helped businesses create training courses for their employees. He knew he wanted to help people through art and, in fact, his dream was very visual. He could quite literally "see" it. He was unsure of how to make the vision real, and he had a bias that the vision was of little value to the world around him. He and I went through the process of discovering the *what* and the *how*. *What is it you want to do and how do you get there?*

His *what* was unyielding—he was a right-brainer. Remember, right-brained people have strong ideas; they can feel it, see it, sing it, dance it, write it, mime it—they are so *in* it. They know that idea in their bones, but they have a hard time expressing it. He hadn't identified the struggle with the how, he hadn't named this as a possible problem; instead, he simply said "no" to his dream and lived with feeling frustrated. He blocked his own success by not separating out the *what* and the *how*.

Once he gained awareness of the *what* and the *how*, and of his own tendency to be over-indexed on the what, he found the right next step. Until then, there had been *no* next step.

A word of additional insight—essential to being aware is also the ability to *not judge*. Allow whatever tendency you might have to be "ok." The tendency is there for good reason, built based on familial or learned experience. Honor it by knowing it is there and learning to be aware of it. Judgment of your first step does not provide value either. Instead, know your first step is just "a step" in a series of steps that, when assembled, are the roadmap of your journey. A step is a step.

In our example, my client wanted to tell personal stories through comics that would encourage, help, and heal people. The first step was tough for him because he did not know how to best distribute the stories—should he use a website? Social media? Other outlets? It was the *how* that slowed him down. But, by separating the *what* from the *how*, he could see this was just a structural glitch and did not equate to failure.

Fast-forward ten years, and he earned a Master's degree in psychology and uses comics to help people connect with their emotions. He is out there practicing right now—living his dream!

# CHAPTER 3:

## Success vs. Goals: What's the difference?

We tend to use the words "success" and "goals" interchangeably. For example, "If I obtain goal X, then I am successful." But in our change framework, there is value in understanding that the two concepts are indeed quite different.

A goal is specific. It could be a relationship: I want more friends. It could be an amount of money: I want to make one million dollars this year. It could be a particular job: I want to be the senior vice president of operations. It could be a state of mind: *I want to be more open. I want to be more flexible. I want to be more spiritual.*

Being clear on your goals is important. If your goal is not clear, the idea behind the goal will notoriously be nebulous as well. For example, if your goal is to "make more money," what does that really mean? Do you have a dollar figure in mind? Is there a specific way you want to earn the money? Is there a date or time you want the money by? Who will you be when you reach your goal? For example, if implied in your goal to earn more money is that you will become a CEO, and you are currently a file clerk, it is essential to understand that you need to do some research on what characteristics and traits are needed so you can begin to formulate a CEO mindset.

Success, on the other hand, might be aligned to a goal—but most often, it is not. Let us revisit the goal to make one million dollars. If I make one million dollars in a year, I obtained my goal, but my goal limited me to only one million dollars. What if there is more? This is because we have personal definitions of success based upon our unique core values. Taking time to understand is essential to ensuring you not only reach a goal, but feel the success along with it. What if my definition of success was connected to the idea that success comes from working extremely hard—meaning working sixty hour weeks and multiple jobs? My journey each Monday to Friday will leave me exhausted. The feeling of exhaustion confirms that I have worked hard, and when I am working hard, I am successful. Does exhaustion really indicate success? I could very well work sixty plus hours a week and not meet any of my goals. Further, it is not a sustainable lifestyle.

Taking time to reflect upon what success means to us is important. Having a "work hard" ethic is great, but it is more likely a part of a series of *integers* that work together to help you obtain and embody success.

Remember our Decision Equation from before? Let's use it again, here, to help us better understand success. Let's make a Success Equation. After exploring success, perhaps I come up with the following integers: quality family time, working hard, ensuring my family has everything they need, plus other success integers. I think you get the idea. What if I looked at each of these integers and applied some "weight" to them. For example, it could look like this: Family Time (#1) + Working Hard (#2) + Family Needs (#3) = Success. What this is <u>not</u> about is judging any of the integers in the formula. It is about being very clear on *what* integers are part of the success formula and how important each integer is.

**SUCCESS EQUATION: SUCCESS INTEGER #1 (WEIGHTED) + SUCCESS INTEGER #2 (WEIGHTED) + SUCCESS INTEGER #3 (WEIGHTED) = SUCCESS**

Again, success may or may not be directly attributed to any one goal. It might be based on something very specific like first-quarter revenue, or it might be based on something that is entirely tribal or learned through my familial settings such as, "Am I providing for my family?" or "Are my kids happy?" It is important to take some time to outline your definition of success and to distinguish between success and goals.

## WHAT DON'T YOU KNOW?

We tend to have an immature understanding of success for ourselves. For example, this can show up as not completely thinking something through, so you have a false concept of how much work is involved. The reverse is true, too. You can falsely assume success will be harder than it really is. In either case, I know the common experience for my clients is a sensation of repetition: feeling like they try but fail, feeling like

**IT IS IMPORTANT TO TAKE SOME TIME TO OUTLINE YOUR DEFINITION OF SUCCESS AND TO DISTINGUISH BETWEEN SUCCESS AND GOALS.**

things are harder than they should be, feeling like success eludes them. It can feel like "Groundhog Day".

It is common to feel fatigued, whereby you stop and start over and over again. Inevitably, there's this feeling of "Here I go again." For example, what if we wanted to get back into shape and, to do so, we wanted to restart a workout routine? How many times have we heard those attempting this share stories of planning, starting, stopping, re-planning, starting, and stopping again. I know from working with my clients, one way to resolve this is to understand our goals and to also understand what success means aligned to those goals. Getting to the gym is actually an outcome of other actions, meaning it is on the right side of the equal sign. Remember our Decision Equation? The act of getting to the gym implies I have made the gym a priority; that I have said "no" to something so I can "yes" to the gym. Breaking down the idea of success like this, into quantifiable integers (the Success Equation), clarifies the work it will take and the measures used to evaluate success, creating an improved likelihood for success to occur. And isn't that what it's all about?

Remember, whenever we say "yes" to something, we are also saying "no" to something else. Are you clear on *what* you desire? Are you paying attention to the things you are saying "no" to? Are you clear, and have you thought through the "yes" or "no" tradeoffs? Are you clear as to the amount of work and the level of effort that you need to feel successful and also obtain your goals?

If you are not clear about the tradeoffs, you increase the probability of experiencing discomfort, dissonance, and the spinning of wheels. Is this the type of journey you really want?

## THE DANGER OF WOO-WOO

Remember my client who wanted to make comics? Our initial conversations around his goals yielded he had a very intuitive feeling that he wanted to convey something through art. He was not so clear on how to make that happen. We spent time unpacking his goal, trying to get as specific as possible. If the goal could be felt, how does it feel? If the goal could be eaten, how does it taste? If the goal could be drawn or painted, what does it look like? If the goal could be captured in a video, what do you see yourself doing? In the video, if you are seen working towards your goal, what is it about your character on screen that is most important to the achievement of the goal? We used quite a bit of humor and play as we walked through each of these questions. True, it felt ridiculous at times, but that ridiculousness was telling us we had judgment about the goal! Let me explain. The series of questions revealed with certainty that the goal was a mix of psychology and art. From there, we talked through "*What does it mean to be successful around that?*" We found that he did not believe, at first, that he could ever be successful with art (comics) and psychology. Before he allowed himself to explore the goal, he had a belief that it was not valuable. From there, it all stopped. No progress. That took some *serious* hashing out: "*Why do you think that using visual arts to help people connect to their emotions and their thoughts doesn't have value?*" In fact, within the field of psychology, it absolutely provides value! Once he and I could meaningfully explore the goal and the idea that success was not obtainable, it was evident he was letting his *goals* get mixed up with his idea of *success*. In truth, he did value the visual arts and using them to help

**BREAKING DOWN GOALS AND SUCCESS WITH ATTENTION TO THE WORDS WE USE IS POWERFUL AND SUPPORTS OUR DAY TO DAY DECISION MAKING. WE USE THESE WORDS TO IDENTIFY OPTIONS THAT WOULD NOT OTHERWISE BE AVAILABLE TO US.**

people. However, that was countermanded by a strong perception that real success only came from traditional "business rigor," the 8-to-5 job in the business world, where there's a very clear concept of what success is. Somehow, "art" did not fit into that definition of success.

Eventually, he spun his idea into a counselling practice based on visual arts therapy. Essential to obtaining this outcome was learning about success. We found that from his familial history and some environmental factors there came a belief that art was less valuable—or even seen as unsuccessful. The reason for this belief is unimportant; in coaching, the emphasis is on understanding that this belief exists so you can take informed, new action. For my client, he had an expression that art was seen as "Woo-Woo" which, for him, meant art was not real work and was seen as a distraction. "Woo-Woo" was such a great term, that I have used it with many of my clients to help them understand how powerful beliefs can stop your goals dead in their tracks. Where do you have a "Woo-Woo" belief that is stopping you from achieving a goal or experiencing success?

## GETTING SPECIFIC

When my client first came to me, his desire to share stories visually to connect people with their feelings was strong. This level of intentional detail is not true for many of my clients. Instead, the idea might be, "I think I'd like to draw stuff." Without specificity of goals, it becomes even harder to understand success. Once you clarify what you want (in this case, to tell a story visually) with what makes you feel successful (being of service, providing support and tools to others), that is when things take hold. That is where your success and goals support each other, instead of getting tangled and confused.

I can relate to the frustration of confounded goals and success on a very deep, personal level. For many years, I did not think the things I am sharing in this book were of significant value to be shared. I believed what I had to say was neither important, new, or relatable. Do you see how I cut myself off with my own "Woo-Woo" attitude? I held a belief that what I had to say was *so* bland I must have nothing of value to share, and interestingly, I was also telling myself that I was so different that no one could connect to my ideas! That is obviously a perspective full of contradiction, serving only to keep me away from my goals. Saying "yes" to coaching gave me the opportunity to work with people one-on-one and receive direct feedback that my ideas are relatable and, in fact, work. That's when things started to click.

## THE JOURNEY TO CLARITY

Please know it is normal to be unclear on your goals. Part of the journey, remember, is to understand the goal as well as the steps to obtain it. Remember the *what* and the *how*? Know that we start with ambiguity, and move towards increased understanding, increased awareness, and increased clarity over time. Know it is a moving target and a constant pursuit, because the more you know, the more expanded your perspective will be. The more expanded your perspective, the more you are capable of seeing, and the more clarity you will require. Embrace the perspective that the journey evolves and unfolds. If you hold the expectation that you must know everything all the time, you set yourself up for disappointment. If you can approach the journey with humility, openness, and a resolve to observe and seek understanding, then you will accomplish more than you could imagine. Even better, be curious! If you are curious, you are more likely to have fun and be motivated. The energy of curiosity within the change framework cannot be underestimated. How are you leveraging your power of curiosity today?

I never thought my goal was to become a change consultant and coach within the tech industry, but as I pursued and explored my definition of goals and success, this is what presented itself and made the most sense. Without curiosity in the pursuit of this goal, it would have been easy to become frustrated. For example, some consulting engagements do not align to my vision; however, they clarify and define what I *do* want. Further, I have had false starts and diversions that caused frustration, but they, too, have served to clarify my goals and success.

I know now that my message is meant to land in a bigger audience and to impact others on a larger scale. My individual client work remains an essential integer in my Success Equation, but I have come to understand there is something about sharing at scale that is also important. I was unaware of this until I started working with my goals and success—being curious, taking chances, saying "yes" to acting on faith, and trusting. Remember, I index heavily on the left-brain, where it is all about process. Knowing this, I allowed myself to explore, through process (the *how*), the act of making choices to share my work and I now have experience from that so as to better inform my vision. When I make a perceived misstep, I know that it is meant to inform me in some critical way. Therefore, my definition of success is actually a combination of both success and failure!

Conversely, I could have required complete clarity *before* taking action—what I would term "analysis paralysis." When I do this, I am not honoring who I really am as a left-brained process (how) person. I create dissonance and frustration because I am going against my natural tendency. Think of it like swimming upstream—you will get where you want to go, but you will be exhausted and tired.

## THE POWER OF WORDS

Typically, the more you understand your goal, the clearer your goal becomes. The more knowledge you have about a goal, the more you are open to looking for additional puzzle pieces, opportunities, and steps that get you closer to your goal. The more open and aware I am, the more potential I have to be observant of opportunity.

Language is one of the greatest tools at our disposal when it comes to clarifying goals. *Words are powerful.* If you are familiar with the Harry Potter series, you know one of the themes is that words are magical. It is true. Whether consciously or not, we create our reality using words. We have familial and social (what I term as tribal) beliefs and biases that reinforce or downplay the importance of words. Internalize this truth: words are powerful. The clearer the words I use to describe my goals, the better. I would add that the better emotionally informed we are of our goals, the more amplified positive outcomes become. I use the word "embody" to represent this emotional connection

**IF YOU ARE CURIOUS, YOU ARE MORE LIKELY TO HAVE FUN AND BE MOTIVATED. THE ENERGY OF CURIOSITY WITHIN THE CHANGE FRAMEWORK CANNOT BE UNDERESTIMATED.**

to goals. How do you embody your goals? What are the emotional and physical components? What emotions do you have about the goal? Are there feelings or sensations in your body related to the goal? When you achieve the goal, how will you be different or what will you need to know to be successful? If your goal is to become a CEO, who will you be as the CEO of your own company, versus the file clerk in someone else's company? Is there a distinction between a CEO for a company your built vs. a CEO for a company someone else built? Does that even matter? Leveraging our curiosity here, how does your goal look, smell, sound, feel, taste? It's a recipe. Let's leverage the algorithm used in the Decision and Success Equations, but modify the integers to see if the algorithm can help us here—a Goal Equation. What I see (visual), what I feel (emotions), and what I know (intellect) help me understand my goal. The goal is to the right of the equal sign. The goal equation might look like this:

**GOAL EQUATION: GOAL INTEGER #1 + GOAL INTEGER #2 + GOAL INTEGER #3 = GOAL.**

The words we choose for each of the integers in the goal equation are powerful in helping us understand (*what*) and make progress towards (*how*) our goal. The combination and specificity of the words together help to intensify the clarity our goal.

The words you use have impact. Consider the goal: "*I want my company to make one million dollars in revenue.*" Do you know why you chose one million? Are there beliefs such as fear or loss of control that inform this number which could be limiting you? The beliefs that lay underneath the words reveal much. Have you heard the phrase, "What is not said is just as important as what is said"? This is absolutely true here, and words become essential to helping us understand the intentionality and unintentionally of our goals. The words and vocabulary you leverage reveal and can subconsciously limit your outcome, so be intentional. Be aware.

One of my clients is a brilliant and a natural CEO. It suits her. She deeply values authenticity, but she finds herself in conflict because her values are not mirrored by some of her external business partners. From a negotiation perspective, my client believes you ask for what is right instead of asking for something more, knowing you will eventually negotiate to a final outcome. Part of the behavior in the negotiation process contradicts her authenticity value. Why ask for something false instead of asking for what is real? To add fuel to the fire, she is a female in a male dominated industry, compounded by a global business environment that excludes women. The net outcome for my client is that she is left to deal with the dissonance of her core values and how to cope with the emotional backlash.

She and I worked to break down goals and success. We defined each, seeking words that best represent the intellectual and emotional elements of her CEO goals and success. We focused on the words that strung together to form her Goal Equation. We found that her value of authenticity was absolutely present; however, there were other words such as tenacious, fierce, compromising, unique, innovative, and so forth. Those words provided us with "more" to work from.

We re-evaluated her current situation. She is the "odd woman out" in a male dominated industry, leveraging a different negotiation approach than what is customary. With that in mind, of course she is going to run up against conflict and at times question herself. It is normal and we all do it. It is human nature to seek out others in the environment doing what you do so you can compare. When that is not available, we begin to fill in the gaps with assumption. This is where our words within the goal equation are powerful. My client is experiencing some pain in the situation and yes, her value of authenticity is in conflict.

This is the opportunity to leverage her other success integers which, prior to the exercise, we did not know were available. She can tap into her fierceness and innovation that are being called to action. What if she communicated that she will not negotiate status quo, but she has another approach she would like to move forward with instead of the back and forth method of the past? Breaking down goals and success with attention to the words we use is powerful and supports our day to day decision making. We use these words to identify options that would not otherwise be available to us.

## EMBODYING YOUR GOALS & SUCCESS

The importance of words has introduced the idea of embodiment. Intentionally defining goals and success with meaningful words provides richness and texture, helping us to viscerally connect to goals and measures of success. Goals and success can be seen as "things," but when we personalize them with characterization and nuance, we are able to better connect with them, embody them, and live them.

This strategy of embodiment is facilitated by visualization, a process that Olympic athletes use all the time. Wanting to be the world's fastest sprinter, I train aggressively. I also visualize my form, my breath, and how I feel at various stages of the race. Clearly visualizing yourself achieving a goal—starting the business you always hoped for, obtaining that new career, crossing that finish line with the ribbon flat across your chest—you teach your inner self to expect it.

Using this technique to explore success, we increase the opportunity to understand our blind spots. Blind spots are the things we consciously or unconsciously ignore, which impact our ability to effectively achieve our goal. Using a map as an example, if a pin on the map represents the goal, can you see the roads you need to take to reach the goal? Will there be traffic, and is it better to take surface streets or an expressway? The map might show the fastest route is by expressway; however, your inclination might be to use surface streets because you have a negative bias (blind spot) towards expressways. Visualization, like our map example, can highlight where you might have a learned bias that might not be apparent otherwise. How much do you leverage visualization for your goals and definition of success?

# CHAPTER 4:

## Your Values, Your Self

Values guide us and support us to make the best, most informed decisions. Values represent what is most important to us, and help us transcend any specific situation. Whatever we need or is missing from our lives, we value. We can leverage values to ensure we make decisions that support our sense of well-being and self-actualization.

Values are an essential part of the human experience, and they grow and mature just as we as physical entities grow and mature. They can expand and contract as we accumulate human experience and, most notably, as we interact with the change framework. Change facilitates outcomes where a value increases its meaning and understanding or conversely decreases and becomes more narrowly focused. I like to think of values as a living part of ourselves.

Values are essential ingredients to the propulsion system of change energy. When we deeply understand our values (and belief systems, which we will talk about later) we can be at choice, consciously moving forward within the change framework. Without a clear understanding of values, it is all too easy to make decisions that lead us away from what we want. It is important to explore values, define them as we understand them to date, explore if they have changed over time, and identify areas where we have false expectations or assumptions, to increase our awareness so as to make decisions and move closer to conscious choice. Doing this shifts us from being uninformed to being informed. Doing this activates change energy to propel us closer to the future state that we envision.

We want to know the "right" step to take when, in fact, there is no right step. There is just "the step" in front of you. A clear set of core values supports the confidence associated with any step and helps discourage the natural urge to judge or evaluate each step as successful or unsuccessful. We have already made the connection in the prior chapter that our values and beliefs serve as a foundation from which we identify goals and define success. Values support and enable our ability to embody the vision we have. Values anchor us, and I like to think of them as a touchstone that we return to again and again to get grounded.

Remember my CEO client from the last chapter? She has a core value around authenticity, and the minute she does not operate from that value she experiences dissonance. Nobody else around her knows that, but she does. The dissonance makes her churn, creating a place where she's stuck reacting to her frustration instead of focusing on the issue at hand. Until she identifies the churning and associated frustration as a symptom of being out of alignment with her values, she's stuck focusing on the churn instead of what is most important. That's why unpacking and understanding values is so essential—it keeps us on track. Are there areas in your life where you arefocusing on the churn factor instead of the heart of the matter?

**WE WANT TO KNOW THE "RIGHT" STEP TO TAKE, WHEN IN FACT THERE IS NO RIGHT STEP.**

Your commitment to continuously understand your values and how they mature helps keep you from getting distracted in the first place. For example, when you start something new, have you connected with your values, understood any tradeoffs, and established a clear understanding of success? As you assess recommendations from friends and family, do you first evaluate the recommendations against your values? Evaluation against values helps to keep you aligned to what is important, and over time, will clarify the why behind your choices. (You will notice that up to this point, we focused attention on understanding the what and the how of our change journey. Progressing forward, our discussion shifts to highlight methods that increase your learning about you so you can become clearer on why you make the choices you do.)

The commitment to understanding core values requires vigilance to proactively manage judgment. In fact, it is best not to judge values. Values are a natural part of who you are, and they grow with you. Understanding values is a good thing; judgment simply creates churn. My values are not better than yours and vice versa. My values guide me, and your values guide you.

When we explore our shared values, we find more shared commonalities than differences, and we confirm we want only the best for one another. If this is true, why do we have so much social conflict? I postulate that our social construct is engineered to distract us so as to keep the time available for self-reflection to a minimum. Additionally, marketing creates a false sense of social norms that become so ingrained in our awareness that we are blind to what is obviously not true. It is pervasive. Taking one area as an example, marketing informs us how we should look—weight, fitness, skin color, clothing, and more. In parallel, we are inundated with fast food commercials and ads for chemically modified foods. There is a huge mismatch, yet we watch the commercial marketing and, by our consumer habits, we endorse the marketing message. The examples are not limited to appearance, but are available in every aspect of our lives—food, health, politics, and so on. The single most impactful thing you and I can do is get aligned to our core values and operate from there. Over time, false beliefs are exposed, truths are understood, and as a collective we create an opportunity for different outcomes. Change starts with you and is driven by what is most important to you.

## SO, WHAT ARE YOUR VALUES?

We bring our values with us into everything we do. Values become the epitaph of who we are. People remember us by our values: "He was a generous person," or "He always asked more of himself than those around him." However, there is a distinction between the legacy of our values and the legacy of our gifts. There are many high profile examples to use, but I will use Steve Jobs for illustrative purposes. Steve is most noted for his gifts to the personal computing world. Today, Apple products have a distinctive look, feel, and level of performance and usability that is unique. This is a fact separate from my personal like or dislike of an Apple product. The technology legacy is Steve's gift. In contrast to the technology gift is his legacy of business values. A lot has been written on how he conducted or misconducted himself in business with his peers. Again, this fact is separate from my own personal like or dislike of Steve. The purpose here is to separate out the "who" from the "what" and look at how core values live beyond you. If someone wrote a book about your gifts separate from how you lived your life against your core values—what would be written?

Allow yourself time to sit and listen to yourself, to be aware of yourself, to hear your inner dialogue, both the inner critic and the inner advocate of your mind. Know that we are the sum composite of the best of the best of ourselves and the worst of the worst of ourselves. Think of it as the yin and yang of who you are. because *it will tell you what your values are.* The inner dialogue is always there for us to discover, but typically we do not provide time to *listen.*

It's easy to see why. As previously mentioned, we have a lot of marketed distractions. It is critical to be curious about the benefits of the distractions. For example, TV might allow me a chance to escape a busy day. Perhaps I am on my phone all day because my day is not very exciting and I am bored. Do I overpost on social media because I have something to say, or am I hoping to be seen? Everything we do, we do because there is something of value—however big or small. We get something out of it. Know that this is a natural part of our world. Understanding this allows us the opportunity to be curious and to appreciate why the distraction is needed. This is not about evaluating the distraction, but about understanding—so that you can be informed and be purposeful. If I am choosing a distraction, I should know why I am choosing it.

What can we do to help us become more aware of distractions, thereby helping ourselves become clearer with our values? If we can provide an interruption

**FIXED BELIEFS ARE LIKE HAVING A MONKEY ON OUR BACK. THEY DISTRACT US AND REDIRECT OUR ENERGY FROM OUR GOALS TO THE MANAGEMENT AND CONTROL OF THE FALSE BELIEF.**

to what can be an automatic response or behavior, we give ourselves the chance to observe and learn. For example, if food is a distraction and you want to better understand that, put a sticky note visibly on your refrigerator or pantry that reads, "*Stop and count to 10.*" Count to ten before you open the refrigerator, because it gives you ten seconds to disrupt what would have been an automatic response for food. It allows you time to get present and get into your body so that you can be curious about what you are doing, to understand your values around this distraction, and understand how it has become a habit. Leave judgment at the door; this is about being curiously observant. Be gentle, because it takes a while to modify distractions that might have gradually formed a habit.

## CORE VS. SHADOW VALUES

Some values are core and part of who we are from a young age. In contrast, some values are created through experience with our familial and social tribes we belong to. These are called shadow values.

For example, my CEO client has a value around authenticity. This value of authenticity could conflict with social beliefs, and she might start to adopt a shadow value—a diluted version of authenticity—so that she can fit into the broader social framework, thereby reducing external conflict. The adoption of a shadow value can go unnoticed. While working on core values with my clients, they uncover the distinction between core and shadow values and where they are or are not living authentically. It becomes clear where social influences have caused them to modify their value so it will fit a social instance. They notice the churn this has caused and where they have inadvertently focused on the churn vs. the heart of the matter.

As we resolve shadow values and refine our overall values, we introduce a change event. To date, those in your tribe have only known you in the context of your existing set of values. The refinement of your values introduces the tribe to a different or new you.

The variance can be minor or extreme, depending on the value and amount of shadow involved. What is consistent is knowing that your tribe will need time to adapt to and accept who you are in response to the modified value. The decisions you make which were once anticipated and familiar to the tribe are now different, to one degree or another, and what once was familiar is new. This nuance can be lost for some, and I have found that paying attention helps foster understanding, positively impacting the relationships that mean the most to us.

Understanding the influence of values—in or out of alignment—as a key mechanism to inform our navigation in the change framework is an essential concept to master. Each type of value provides context, experience, and perspective from which we learn. How do we truly understand our values across the many contexts of our lives—work, home, and social? Those are experiences that ultimately help us to better understand and mature our value system. As stated before, essential to all of this is our ability to be curious. Curiosity allows us to be inquisitive and non-judgmental.

## THE TRANSACTION OF VALUES

Our core values quite normally bump into one another. Understanding your values as a system enables you to manage competing values. A very simple example might be the following: if you value friendship, but you also value family, what do you do when a sibling's graduation is the same day as a best friend's wedding? When this happens—and the reality is, it happens in one form or another daily—you make tradeoffs. Remember, when you say "yes" to one thing, you're saying "no" to something else. We are always saying "yes" or "no." "Yes" to my next two hours to write this book means "no," I'm not going to work with that client. I highly

**SOLICITING FEEDBACK FROM THOSE WHO KNOW YOU BEST, AS WELL AS A BROADER CIRCLE, WILL HELP INFORM YOUR GOAL AND DISMANTLE FALSE BELIEFS.**

value my one-on-one work with my clients, and I derive an immense amount of satisfaction from that work; but to write, I must make a satisfaction tradeoff. The more clarity I have of my values behind the tradeoff, the more I reduce the possibility of future dissonance or conflict. Fast-forward ahead two months, it is hard to be angry with myself for having less one-on-one client time when I made an informed choice from the get-go to write the book.

Understanding that I have many core values, and that they operate as a system, the more I am purposefully powerful with my in-the-moment decisions. We each have a hierarchy of values, and the choices we make depend on both the contextual situation and the hierarchy of our value system.

## USING VALUES TO MAKE DECISIONS

The more time we devote to exploring values, the more we understand how they operate as a system. The exploration supports our general awareness so we can bring our values forward in everyday life. Is exploration enough? No. Science tells us we need to have reminders to trigger new habits. In this case, we want to support the accessibility of our values. You wear a bracelet that says "Love" to ensure decisions or actions come from a loving place. Some people journal about their values because the act of journaling supports their awareness mechanism. Whatever the practice, the outcome remains the same—ensuring decisions are informed by values increases our odds of being purposeful.

My move to the Pacific Northwest is an example, which I touched on earlier. I chose a region where it rains a lot, and even though I knew it would be rough, I said "yes" to the move based on the understanding of my values. In this case, I had a value of trust—specifically, trusting my intuition. My intuition told me to move despite others telling me not to move or that there was no need to move. Knowing my values and trusting my intuition, I was able to say "yes" to relocating to a rainy place with full consciousness of what I was getting into. More importantly, I knew my values, so when I suffered because of the rain, it wasn't random, and I did not feel the need to blame. Blame would have created a negative experience, wasting time and energy for myself and those around me.

To be clear, this didn't mean the decision was simple or easy. There were times when I was in the Pacific Northwest thinking, "This weather is depressing." And it was depressing from time to time, but from my informed choice, I now had an opportunity to see it as beautiful. I learned I love winter, because where I had previously lived in California, I rarely had a real winter, never experiencing the depth of all four seasons. Because I allowed myself to have that understanding, I could see beauty where I was. *I made an informed decision instead of feeling acted upon.* There came an opportunity to learn. There is always something to learn if we choose to seek it.

## BOXED-UP IN BELIEFS

Thus far we have talked explicitly about values, but what about beliefs? Beliefs are based on context, history, and interpretation of life experience. Beliefs are assumptions we hold to be true. Decisions based on beliefs assume that the causal relationships of the past, which led to the belief, will apply in the future. I, and many others, agree that the rapidly changing and complex world makes using information from the past to make decisions about the future to be risky. I would add that most of us view history with a bias—consciously or unconsciously—preventing us from accurately representing all sides of the historical story.

Although not ideal, the fact of the matter is, we use beliefs to navigate through life. With that in mind, how can we leverage beliefs strategically? We have already used a map as an analogy for helping us expose our blind spots while navigating to a goal. The purpose of the map is to provide a framework to assist us in finding our orientation; what is true north, for example. Suspending judgment, any navigation—even if it based on a false or ill-informed belief of "true north"—is better than nothing. I truly believe that taking a step, even if ill-informed, will lead me to the next step where I can learn more about the belief and any flaws it might have. That learning will inform the next decision, and so on. There is a buildup of learning, course corrections happen, and the belief transforms.

When we lock down our belief systems, we erode our ability to course correct. This is more common than not. As a tribe, we are wired to seek out consistency amid all the volatile societal changes. In this process, beliefs and values get befuddled, and beliefs become fixed. When operating from a fixed belief system, you might say, "*All Catholics do this. All Protestants do that. All Arab countries do this. All EU countries do that.*"

But we know, when we break that logic down, those generalizations never pan out.

Our beliefs are based on context and experience. The more openly we hold that, the healthier our beliefs will be. Beliefs are meant to evolve, change, and adapt. The minute you stop growth, you create dissonance and constrain your change journey. We have talked about the concept of "Groundhog Day" in the prior sections, and constrained beliefs are another area that cause us to repeat experiences until we are ready to let go and learn.

Let's look at three example beliefs that commonly impede progress:

*The belief that my idea is not good enough.* As we generate ideas, it is quite natural for us to compare. We look around ourselves for others who are doing or have done something similar, building in our minds a false scale from which we devalue our idea. The fact of the matter is, if you had the chance to talk with the owner of the other idea, they would most likely share they doubted their idea, too. That said, tipping the scale in the other direction and holding your idea to be bigger than it is can be troublesome as well. So there needs to be a balance. Soliciting feedback from those who know you best, as well as a broader circle, will help inform your goal and dismantle false beliefs.

*The belief that I will fail* can be based on historical experience that is being misapplied to the current goal. The reason why we failed in the past would not necessarily be the reason we fail now. Failure can be projected from those around us based on reasons that have nothing to do with us. Someone could be jealous, for example, and in their jealousy, project failure onto you. Cast a wide net for feedback and ask questions around similar efforts in the past where you might have had skill gaps. Use discernment to review the feedback, taking into consideration the bias—positive or negative—of the person providing the feedback.

**EACH AND EVERY EXPERIENCE YOU CREATE FOR YOURSELF IS AN OPPORTUNITY TO LEARN, NO MATTER WHAT DIRECTION IT IS IN, AND LEARNING IS AN ESSENTIAL PART OF THE CHANGE PROPULSION FRAMEWORK.**

*The belief that no one else has the same problem.* I saved the best for last. Almost every client has some aspect of their belief system that tells them they are the only ones experiencing whatever it is they are experiencing. The moment I share three or four examples of others tackling the same problem, albeit in a different context, they sigh in relief. "You mean I am not the only one?"

Fixed beliefs are like having a monkey on our back. They distract us and redirect our energy from our goals to the management and control of the false belief.

A good test of whether you are working with your beliefs in a healthy way is how you respond when they are challenged. Do you respond based on historical knowledge or with current facts? Do you respond out of anger or love? Do you respond with fear or with courage? The truth is, your beliefs can help you pivot your journey. Allow curiosity to help you understand your beliefs and where they could be more informed and better understood.

## WHAT ARE YOUR BELIEFS?

As you did with values, give yourself space to sit and listen to yourself. Reflect back, as far as you can go, to examine the beliefs you might have. Write them down. Acknowledge each of us is unique and has skills that others don't in areas of art, music, math, and the like. I tell my clients to paint it, draw it, sing it, mime it—just get it down on paper and work with it! Humor aside, the idea is to get your beliefs out of your thoughts and on paper so you can see them and interact with them. There is a difference between just thinking about them and actually working with them on paper. Beliefs, as with values, typically do not get a lot of time to be explored on their own; instead, we wait until there is a problematic situation and we are forced to work with them.

Let's work with some sample beliefs. "All cops are the good guys," or conversely, "all cops are bad guys." "9/11 was perpetrated by terrorists," or conversely, "9/11 was a false-flag operation." Depending upon your personal life experience, you will have a powerful attraction to these beliefs. I used these particular examples on purpose because they are super-charged and typically ignite something within us. Less-charged beliefs might be "orange is the best color," or conversely, "red is the best color."

Beliefs are not always fun or easy to explore; it can be a bumpy ride. The difficulty comes when new information challenges the historical view and, in so doing, breaks down the logical framework used to build a worldview from which decisions are made. There is a challenge to rethinking what you thought was factual. What things have you said "yes" to without ever really considering why? Saying "no" to something that you've said "yes" to your whole life now could potentially make you an outsider to your established tribe. So, another part of this reflection is asking, *are you okay with being different*?

Take the time, work with your beliefs, and get an understanding of them. Know how they have evolved and changed; know they will continue to evolve and change. You will be building a perspective that allows you to make informed decisions and, more importantly, to understand *when* you make a decision based on a value or a belief. Remember, saying "yes" to one thing is always saying "no" to something else.

When we know that, we have power over our own lives.

## WHY THIS MATTERS-
## HOW BELIEFS & VALUES IMPACT SUCCESS

Remember, the definition of success and what success feels like are personal to you. The time invested to understand our values informs us to better understand what about success is important to us. Is it obtaining the goal or is it something we do along the way to obtaining the goal? Beliefs are a natural part of who we are, and ensuring we have the perspective that beliefs change and evolve provides a space of opportunity which otherwise would not be available to us. Knowing we can capitalize on modifying our beliefs, that they are not static, is an opportunity we should always take. That is a giant step towards true success, however you measure it.

# Chapter 5: The Great Lie

There is one more particularly insidious belief I want to touch on. This belief warrants a whole chapter to itself, because almost everyone has fallen prey to it—and it really messes things up. If as a tribe, we can allow this belief to evolve and change, our individual experience in our own change journeys will be greatly transformed. That belief is the idea that progress is only linear. That somehow, success only happens in a forward, linear sequence. Anything other than a forward linear motion means you must be failing.

As a tribe, we pass to each generation the belief that progress is linear, even though we know it to be untrue. The belief is, however, deeply ingrained. It is reinforced in many ways, but fundamentally through religious and religious-based social paradigms, where enlightenment is achieved through an ascension process. I single out this mechanism only because religious paradigms cross all cultures and all continents. Our idea of progress is spiritually and religious-based, whether we realize it or not. We take that on as a paradigm, even if it's not necessarily of service to us. Like breathing or blinking our eyes, the belief becomes a factual part of our world view.

The truth is, the belief is never of service to us, because outside of that spiritual paradigm, it just isn't true. *Progress is not linear.* Progress is a squiggly line; up close, it looks more like a ball of yarn than a smooth-rising graph.

If we analyze "progress," we realize it is a whole series of steps: left, right, front, and back. The steps, when strung together, map us to our goals. We create conflict for ourselves when we assume any decision or step is not part of a perfect linear trajectory. We end up focusing on this personal conflict instead of the task at hand. We miss out on the learning the experience is providing.

## WHY IT MATTERS

Embracing the perspective "progress is not linear" allows us to appreciate our worst selves just as much as our best selves. Using our Decision Equation, progress is the *outcome* of forward, backward, left, and right motion (the Decision Integers). We could write it out like this:

Left + Right + Backward + Forward = Progress. Our shared tribal belief contains a bias that progress is predominantly *linear*, which implies the directions left, right, and backward are negative or inferior in some way. I counter this with the belief that each direction, or integer, contains a valuable learning experience for us. If I miss the learning from any one of these integers, I stunt my learning and force the universe to create other experiences to replace what was lost. This is another culprit behind the sensation of feeling stuck, or experiencing the same problem repeatedly.

**TAKE NOTE WHEN YOU MAKE DECISIONS BASED ON HABITS OR BELIEFS INSTEAD OF CORE VALUES. MAINTAIN GRATITUDE AND REFRAIN FROM JUDGEMENT.**

Working with my clients, we remove the negative bias and focus on the learning—we clear the path for experiencing all four of the integers. The removal of judgment provides a safe place to talk through why it was important to take a step back, left, or right. What did that step provide that a step forward did not?

The volume of self-flagellation imposed by taking any step other than a step forward continues to surprise me. When talking with my clients, they will admit that at a cognitive level they know taking a step back is valuable, but it becomes clear the opposing social belief creates a very real struggle.

Each and every experience you create for yourself is an opportunity to learn, no matter what direction it is in, and learning is an essential part of the change propulsion framework.

## STUCK IN OUR BELIEFS

I know many readers are going to get stuck here. The idea of progress as anything other than linear will create a significant challenge. I am confident that if you feel resistance to the challenge I am proposing here, ask yourself if you are experiencing recurring problems or frustrations over and over. The tricky thing is, *you don't know what you don't know until you know it.* If you don't let go of the belief that progress is linear, it will be hard to realize the total value of its opposite. It is a bit of a conundrum. If you are not willing to see holes in an existing belief, it will be hard to believe or even understand what can be different by having a new or alternate belief.

This happens with a lot of beliefs, of course. We get stuck in them. We fight the idea of change. As an example and to be provoking—what if I hate a particular ethnicity, and if you are that ethnicity, then I am going to hate you. I won't care who you are as a person. You could be the greatest dad, the greatest mom, the greatest friend; but you are of that race, and if I hate all people of that race, I cut myself off from any opportunity to learn or grow, and I am severely stunted as a result.

## BACKWARDS PROGRESS IN MY OWN LIFE

I have had a first-hand opportunity to learn that progress is something other than a smooth, linear, forward-progressing line. In the foreword, I shared one of the very first memories I had as a child and the promise I made to myself to always find a way. Fast-forward to my early twenties, well into the journey of finding my way, and I was at the precipice of a giant decision. It was Christmas, and after a series of events, it was clear I needed to separate from my family—particularly my mom. The decision went against everything I had ever been taught and was contrary to any forward, linear progression I had known. Although it felt uncomfortable, I decided to call a timeout. It took about a decade, but eventually, I reconnected with my mom. When I first reconnected with her by phone, she heard my voice but did not know who I was. We talked for a half-hour before she finally figured out it was me. Today, we can connect openly and have a great relationship. This taught me that there are moments when we cannot move forward without moving back, and that moving back (or left or right) is subjective. The act of separation (which seemed counterintuitive) created a space for something to happen for each of us that would not have happened otherwise. From that point forward, I no longer believed in progression the same way.

# Chapter 6:
## Is Change a Journey - Or a Destination?

The concept of change being a journey and not a destination may or may not be "news." However, I believe many of us forget this concept as we quite naturally get swept up in the individual moments of the journey. The perceived criticality in those moments can blind us to the bigger picture. That said, it becomes important to find balance; living in the moments of the journey as well as leveraging the moments to take a step back to gain perspective. Know that the journey is filled with sprints and marathons and, like an athlete, you must train accordingly. Goals are meant to guide the journey, and as soon as we complete one goal, another soon reveals itself.

We have seen previously that we can be over-indexed on the how of a decision. Likewise, we can inadvertently over-index on our goals. If we are not careful enough, the goal itself can become the sole focus, and experiential learning is lost. Observation is our friend as it helps us identify expectations, habits, and beliefs, creating an opportunity to develop new perspectives from which we can make informed choices. *When we are at choice we are at power.*

If we fixate and focus on the details of the moment and, in the throes of laboring ourselves forward, we do not step back to observe, we miss the opportunity to see ourselves in the sequence of moments that make up the journey towards this goal. How can we remind ourselves to do that? How do you do that for yourself? Is it a string thoughtfully wrapped around your finger, or a sticky note intentionally placed on your laptop lid to remind you to step out of the intensity of the moment to see the big picture? Is it a reminder placed on your electronic calendar alerting you twice daily, "Where are you right now?"

Learn to recognize for yourself where and when you are not consciously at choice. Take note when you make decisions based on habits or beliefs instead of core values. Maintain gratitude and refrain from judgment. Simply observe when and where it happens, and if possible, look for themes, trends, and tendencies. Write down your observations to account for them. Then, play with various methods, finding those that work best for you so that you can intentionally increase moments of observation.

As you move through the process, know that failure is part of the learning. We all learn from polarization; meaning we learn from both positive and negative events. It is normal. I ask my clients to ponder two circumstances: would you learn more from winning the lotto or from going bankrupt? The fact is we learn different lessons from each, and judgment does not serve you in this regard. That said, we cannot cast judgment away and hope for the best. Instead, welcome it with open arms, acknowledging its importance and value. Like a best friend, it can inform us about our

**WHEN WE ARE AT CHOICE WE ARE AT POWER.**

blind spots and where there is learning to be had. This takes a considerable bit of practice, and it helps to have someone, like a coach, to work with you to build your observation muscles so you in turn can build awareness, perspective, and choice.

## FINDING THE DIFFERENCE

Say that I'm focusing on getting a promotion at work. That's my goal. If I am solely focused on the promotion,

I might miss the learning that comes from being on the journey to the promotion. I like to think of learning in two "levels."

Level one is my goal and the steps I need to take to achieve it. Level two is who I am as I am taking those steps, and who I am when I obtain or reach the goal. The promotion is about the new job, the new salary, and maybe the recognition, or perhaps knowing it is an intermediate stepping stone to something else. Underneath, who am I as I initiate my journey to seek and obtain the promotion? Am I confident? Do I know I have the skills or do I know I have gaps that I need fill? If there are gaps, am I unconsciously or consciously giving off signals to those who make the promotion decision that I have or lack confidence based on them? As I acquire knowledge and information to fill any gaps, how does that change me?

If I am myopically focused on the promotion from job A to job B, then I miss the moments in the journey and how I am changing to become and embody the person required for the new job. It becomes essential to balance our attention on the tasks as well as the overall journey so we can better capture who we are in the moments of the journey, bringing awareness to our own personal transformation.

It's a subtle, but important difference. Neither level is more important than the other; you need both to be successful, just like you need both halves of the brain. It is about being very rational and intuitive. Long-term success is found when you balance both attention to the moment and observation of the broader journey. We know balance is not achieved 100% of the time; instead, it ebbs and flows. Our power comes from our ability to be observant, to know we have choice, and to exercise that choice in an informed way.

**TAKE NOTE WHEN YOU MAKE DECISIONS BASED ON HABITS OR BELIEFS INSTEAD OF CORE VALUES. MAINTAIN GRATITUDE AND REFRAIN FROM JUDGEMENT.**

## SUCCESS VS. GOALS REVISITED

This idea of being informed and being of choice as we look at the concept of journey vs. destination compels us to reflect, again, upon the distinction between success and goals. As we position ourselves between knowing the destination and being clear on our goals, part of our clarity is intimately tied to our understanding of what success means to us.

As we discussed prior, goals and success are two very separate concepts that become confounded. We can achieve the goal but still feel unsatisfied and unfulfilled. This can be for an array of reasons such as inflated expectations of the goal, or misapplied historical experience that was never scrutinized for truth.

If we operate between identifying a destination goal and driving to that goal, vacillating between objectivity and being in the moment, our awareness of what success means becomes critically important. If operating from an outdated or inflated understanding of success, we have increased the opportunity to incorrectly define the goal and destination, as well as to make ill-informed decisions.

What if success, for me, was tied to the amount of work or effort I put into a goal? Meaning that if I felt something came easy or that I did not work hard, yet the outcome was that I obtained my goal, I might feel good about the achievement, but that feeling would be minimized in comparison to the same result achieved by working feverishly hard. Taking this understanding and applying it to the destination vs. the journey, we create an opportunity to be more informed, more aware.

As I identify my goal and plot my course, I also keep in mind any bias towards the success of that goal. Notice I am separating out the goal itself from how I will know I am successful in reaching that goal. Through the separation, I can ensure that my goals are not accidently skewed because of an ill-formed definition of success itself. This is how we "create an informed experience."

It's true that along the journey, my bias towards success will inform me to feel good or feel inadequate about my progress towards my goal based on, in this example, how many hours put in or the level of effort applied. Those feelings could lead me to make different decisions or forgo valid, alternative decisions that might render a better outcome. The unconscious bias I have for success can make the journey harder or longer and even make the actual outcomes we seek harder to get.

Again, it becomes essential to encourage and promote that omnipotent observer within you. We all have a tendency towards one side of the brain or another—to be more rational or more intuitive. The awareness of our tendency helps us maintain balance. How do you push yourself forward to the goal (level 1), while also sustaining awareness (level 2) of how our values impact our view of success and play an important role in triggering or inhibiting choice? Simply operating from the perspective that awareness is essential and required is the first step. If you fundamentally accept that awareness is required, you will do your best to create awareness when it is needed. If and when it wanes, you will leverage curiosity to understand why and course correct. Leaving judgment at the door, you will learn about any habits or beliefs that no longer serve you. You will create space for new understanding and knowledge, and from that will build choice and create opportunities for new outcomes. Awareness and understanding can help you thrive on that second level.

An airline pilot's idea of a successful flight can be based on many different goals. It could include timeliness, comfort, or safety, and it can equally include elements such as maneuvering a tough flight schedule, demonstrating leadership, the ability to connect to the crew, or positive impressions on customers. Each is valid. Our pilot is preparing for a flight from Chicago to LA, and initiates all the normal pre-flight processes, procedures, and protocols. The flight encounters weather and turbulence. The pilot realizes winds have taken them slightly off their original flight plan. She makes a course correction. Radar indicates unforeseen weather accumulating, which will necessitate a diversion. She makes a course correction. There is increasing turbulence at the current altitude. She makes a course correction. The flight lands in LA almost an hour later than anticipated. She loves to see the passengers deplane, so she stands at the front to say goodbye and thank them for flying. The response from the customers is mixed. Some are happy, some are frustrated, some are late. The captain finally departs and, as she does, she remembers her goal of a safe flight. Deep down, she is happy because she got everyone to their destination safe and sound. But deeper down, she does not feel like celebrating. Some of the looks she received from the deplaning customers had her second-guessing. She realizes she had another value—she wanted to please the customers. As she continues towards the hotel for her layover, she thinks back upon historical events from her young adulthood— when she learned that by pleasing, she felt good. Boarding the bus for the hotel, she thinks about how she got more than 200 people safely to LA and how great that felt. Maybe it was okay for the customers to have a different perspective on success. In fact, knowing all of the decisions she had to make to keep them safe would cause them more duress than simply being late. She smiles. She attained a new perspective on success.

## NESTING YOUR GOALS

A Russian nesting doll has many dolls stacked inside one another. Our goals are like that. If you have a big goal, perhaps to be CEO, then the path to that goal is full of smaller goals stacked inside of each other. For example, a college student takes a summer consulting internship in hopes of getting hired after graduation. The associate consultant might want to move up to become a principal consultant. The tenured consultant wants to start their own consultancy business, growing from a one-person shop to being a CEO of thousands. Our goals exist in the context of bigger goals; sometimes we can see this, and sometimes we cannot. If we cannot, it can be because either we cannot or do not want to.

It is easy to reflect back upon our journey to draw out the broader themes from what seemed to be rapidly changing events. It is quite different to be in the middle of the journey with the intent to be curious about the bigger picture.

Always ask yourself what you are intentionally planning for. It is okay and quite natural to respond with, "I don't know." Be keen that not knowing does not mean something is wrong or that you are doing something wrong. Don't allow not knowing to create fear or a false problem which causes you to not want to evaluate the bigger picture. Maybe you are simply focused on trying to figure out the next step; maybe you don't know your macro (bigger) goal. There is power in identifying and giving a name to what you don't know. The first step is to become aware of what you don't know, then begin to work with it, allow it to grow, all the while leveraging curiosity to build more knowledge and understanding. Curiosity propels us forward. Saying "I should know," or "I am stupid for not knowing," keeps us stuck.

Settling into curiosity, instead of judgment, when we do not know our macro goal, helps us to be at ease with change. The people closest to us, the friends and family who love us most, can help us be at ease or unease with our judgment. For example, they could have an idea of what they think our macro goal should be, and although they might have good intentions, they can act in a way that creates some friction for us. The reverse is true as well—our friends and family can help us see the bigger version of ourselves that, for whatever reason, we cannot see for ourselves. Leveraging feedback along with our own sense of knowing and trusting becomes the dance of our journey; the dance of our life. It remains important to step out of the moment, be observant, and make the determination of what is known and unknown about your goals. The power is in the observation. Once you observe, you are then able to inform, understand, be curious, and create the opportunity for new perspective, new choice, and new outcomes. This shift facilitates a deeper understanding of who you are and that this is just as much about the journey as it is about the destination. That allows you to rest in the journey, to not stress about "What's the next step?" or "What am I doing?" That's all about the destination.

If you can harness this understanding and the power of this perspective, the shift will be with you from this day forward.

## HOW I FOUND CHANGE

I had the fortunate experience of working with my own coach, who shared her intuitive perspective that my life's work will be meaningful and publicly visible. She was confident my work would be unique, resonant, recognizable, and reach many people across many cultures. She saw something in me that I did not see for myself, yet.

The vision challenged me. At the time, coaching had not become a clearly defined career goal. I am very private person. I did not want to be out on public display, to be that vulnerable or that available to people. Her vision went beyond what I was comfortable with at the time.

In hindsight, I did not deny the perspective she had. It felt right. The expanded view took me out of my comfort zone, though. In my true, right-brained approach, I focused on the short-term tasks at hand where I was most comfortable. I began to focus on my immediate employment circumstances and where I needed to invest in myself to move forward.

I went back to school for my Master's degree, and obtained a few certifications in areas like project and change management. Over time, the scope of my work began to move beyond working with business change to working with people and their change. Soon, I became certified as a coach. The work transitioned, almost naturally, from helping teams deliver projects to helping teams work together to deliver projects. Somewhere along the way, people who I worked with asked me to work with them one-on-one. Please know that in the beginning, I had no desire to be a coach, let alone an understanding of what professional coaching was. Years later, the vision someone else saw so clearly became real. Because I have done the work along the way, I know it could have gone no other way. I confess my fears kept me from taking big steps early on and restrained me to only the immediate next steps. And that is okay. Over time, I looked beyond the near-term to the longer-term and slowly inched my way to the bigger vision. The journey helped me embrace the uncomfortable destination, and curiosity fueled my experience.

I have a better understanding today of what my mentor meant when she said our work would be similar in some ways. Like my mentor, I transparently share the bigger vision that is available to my clients, and I hold that vision even when they either don't want to or are unable to. The power of our perspectives to inform and provide choice and opportunity embodies the journey. Someone helped me to understand that, and it changed my life. Now I have the honor to do the same for others.

As my work evolved from primarily business-centric program and change management to working with individuals and their personal relationship with change, I became acutely aware that I could observe gaps and opportunities my clients could not see for themselves. My clients were not broken or deficient, but instead, due to situational circumstances, they were temporarily impaired, unable to see what was available to them. Whether business or individual, my clients are incredibly focused on going from point A to point B, and when I work with them, they begin to see other options and unlock their own creative solutions.

Today, I make little distinction between the corporate or individual work. There is, of course, variation of context, as there are slightly different rules in the corporate world compared to our lives outside of work. Yet there are more similarities between the two that make jumping back and forth intuitive—and at the same time fun.

Whether corporate or individual, it can be difficult for the client to grasp the whole picture due to current circumstances. It feels overwhelming, like "untangling a ball of yarn." The first step is to notice there is a tangled mess—to name it and begin to work with it. What do we think the problem is? And within it, what things are intertwined and confounded? As we begin the process of untangling, it becomes clear that bias based on history and assumption has ill-informed the current situation so that what we assume to be true is not. Pulling back the strands of yarn, one by one, and asking informed questions based on observation leads to new understandings, new perspectives, and new choices, the game changes and so does my client.

Coaching is not for the faint of heart. Most situations are emotionally charged. Having had my own experience helps me to jump into the journey to join my client right where they are, in the thick of it. My clients are ready to dig deep and say "yes" to change in a way they have not done in the past. The blame game no longer works—in fact, they are exhausted by it. They are focused on what they need to know to turn their current experience upside down, making changes that carry them forward in a substantial way.

# Chapter 7
## The 'You' in Change

What framework do you leverage for change, and what perspectives do you hold about change that work for you and against you?

The structure of this book is intentional. We began with the change framework and introduced concepts like the algorithm that produced the Decision, Progress, and Goal Equations. These tools equip us to better understand and leverage change. We used contrasting concepts such as goals versus success and journey versus destination, drilling down below the surface to become curious with perspectives. Having read the book thus far, what is your perspective of success and goals? Is it different than you originally thought? Are you noticing any perspective shifts? What do you know about yourself that you did not know before? In every chapter, we dug deeper and used repetition to reinforce concepts. Research shows we need to have items repeated seven to ten times to support learning. I believe this is particularly true when what we are changing is so deeply infused as how you breathe or when you blink your eyes.

In this chapter, we purposely pull back and re-orient ourselves to the framework level. Use the framework to explore the proposed idea that change is a naturally-occurring development and should not be feared or avoided. It is merely a process and can be seen as a propulsion mechanism providing you a methodology to navigate today through to tomorrow. It seeks to inform and educate you about *you* to better understand values, clarify beliefs, and break down assumptions.

You are not the goal, but instead, the goal provides the journey with a "north star," facilitating learning, and supporting you to be at choice; at one with your power. Any one goal we have is so much more than just the act of obtaining the goal. If you forget that, you are robbed of the richness of the total experience. Who you are before, during, and once you have attained your goal are essential to foster understanding, learning, and personal and professional development.

## ACHIEVING YOUR GOAL

Based on our conversation thus far, we can see that change is an outcome of the relationship between you and your goals. And as you get further along your journey, it is typical for your goals to change and evolve as you change and evolve.

Let's revisit the goal of aspiring to become a CEO. Very early on, as you plan your goal and start to envision it, you will quite normally make some assumptions about the role. For example, you might think you will act or be a certain way. Maybe there is an element of control and power, of knowing the answers, of being answerable to no one. Maybe there is a CEO role model you have identified, and who is the basis for your assumptions about the role.

**THE MORE YOU LEARN, THE MORE YOU ARE INFORMED AND ABLE TO ACQUIRE NEW PERSPECTIVES THAT PROVIDE OPPORTUNITY FOR NEW CHOICE AND NEW OUTCOMES.**

Some assumptions may be true. As your journey to becoming a CEO unfolds, your understanding of the goal and who you are within the goal becomes informed. For example, maybe you have more autonomy, but now you are scrutinized in different ways by your employees, the industry, or the media. Where you once thought you would know everything, you find yourself in unfamiliar territory. And you might have more autonomy, but you also have different rules to live by. This newly informed perspective can be learned gradually or can be abrupt, depending upon the journey leading up to it.

This gets to the essence of the personalization of change work, which is the embodiment of the journey we have been speaking about. When we understand the difference between the journey and the goal, and we are able to fully invest in the journey, we have more opportunity to viscerally understand all aspects of the change. I believe failing to do this is one reason why some people achieve their goals but remain unfulfilled.

## CHANGE REALLY ISN'T HARD

When I say change isn't hard, I know I am contradicting popular tribal sentiment. However, change is simply a mechanism, a propulsion tool to get us from here to there. That is it. What *is* difficult is the observation and learning needed, and when our beliefs and assumptions countermand our learning, creating dissonance and difficulty.

A plane's flight plan requires updates during the flight, doesn't it? If you literally just hard-coded the straight line from Chicago to LA, you'd be in trouble. That's not how flight works. You have headwinds, drifts, storms, and air traffic control. You must adjust.

Embodying change means mapping that journey in real time. If I am in destination-mode, I won't notice that I am drifting and need to re-orient. The more you learn about being a CEO, the more you might realize you don't want that role at a Fortune 100 company. Maybe your personality would work better leading organically at a startup. Maybe you realize it is the idea of leading something new to market that created the excitement within you all the while, and you don't want to be a CEO at all! That's not something you want to learn at the finish line—that's something you want to pick up along the way, and adjust accordingly.

Let's revisit the statement: *You don't know what you don't know until you know it.* The power of that moment—when you realize what was assumed is no longer true or what you thought you fully understood is not understood—is difficult to express in words. Depending on the magnitude, it can be life changing. How you capitalize on that moment of learning and play it forward is the engine behind change as an energy source.

## HOW CHANGE SUPPORTS MOMENTUM

If all this is true, we can be confident that within the change framework we will progressively move in the direction of our goals and aspirations. But to really take advantage of the change framework, to embody change, you need to have a learning mindset—seeking to learn more about *who you are.*

The dualities, such as goals and success or values and beliefs, are the tools to facilitate your learning more about you. Playing with those dualities will help you zoom in on who you are in any moment. That's important, because you will never be the same person you were when you set the goal. You will always change, and keeping that awareness of who you are at key moments supports you to be as aware as you can be, so you can live the journey to its fullest. This is not a maybe; it's a certainty. Every one of my clients has learned something about themselves that informs how they approach a specific aspect of life, a specific circumstance, differently. It bears repeating: The more you learn, the more you are informed and able to acquire new perspectives that provide opportunity for new choice and new outcomes.

## THE OUTCOME WE ALL HOPE FOR

The truth is, there is a universal outcome we all yearn for. Intuitively, we know that experiencing life from a state of fear, despair, frustration, or even hate does not serve us well. It reinforces the feeling of isolation and separation. We are our best selves when we are at peace, confident, learning, and grounded in love for ourselves and those around us.

If you opened this book, there's a fair chance something isn't happening in your life. When we feel stuck, or don't know what our next step is, we seek solutions and answers to our questions. When we sense something imminent, something looming, we naturally try to anticipate and prepare for what it might be. It is quite normal, and it is how we are wired to react—it is how we survive. As we navigate from today to tomorrow, we strive to do so with grace and ease. Knowing there is a universal process at work here, for me, is soothing and calming. I no longer feel that I must have every answer for every question completely figured out. Instead, I can rest assured that the change framework will support me. My sole job is to be a good participant, a good learner and, most of all, to have fun along the way. This book is not a 10-step program where by completing the steps everything comes together perfectly. It is about understanding the change framework, realizing your active participation within it, and knowing that realizing goals is great, but what we gain from the experience striving for the goal is better. It is about clarifying goals, success, values, and beliefs so that you can really leverage them effectively.

In this book, I have used several examples to represent very real themes and outcomes experienced by my clients and how using the change framework helped them to be informed, to learn, and to shift perspectives. Without the change framework, we work hard to attain goals, but are not fulfilled. Know that your relationship with change directly impacts your change outcomes, goal attainment, and fulfillment and happiness!

# CONCLUSION

## The Steps Are Now

This book has been a journey in its own right. We started by understanding the structure of change and our role in the change framework. Being in this framework, we have access to momentum, movement, and power. We learned how challenging existing perspectives can shine a light on who we are and who we can become.

You do not have to have the details of the master plan completely laid out. Instead, focus on being the best observer of yourself that you can be. By engaging in thoughtful introspection, and by working with the change framework, you are embodying the change you want. There is no secret next step, only the next step. This book is not meant to spur you towards one specific goal; it is meant to be read and re-read, because you *don't know what you don't know until you know it.* The first read might provide the new understanding and shifts that are unique and applicable only to you. You will leverage the learnings to form new perspectives, thereby pivoting your own change journey. Each time you return to this book, there will be something new, even though no new words were added. As you apply what is here, you will naturally make room for more understanding. That is how this book is meant to work. Come back, revisit, and continue to learn.

The more we engage, observe, and incorporate our learnings to inform future decisions, the more personal power we have. The power helps us to forgo the lies, "I can't do that. The world doesn't see me as valuable. My perspective doesn't matter." Those lies rob us of our power. The truth is, if you realize your voice matters, you need not be confounded by journey and circumstance; all you need to do is engage, observe, and learn. You can be at choice and know your power.

**YOU DO NOT HAVE TO HAVE THE DETAILS OF THE GRAND PLAN COMPLETELY LAID OUT. INSTEAD, THIS IS ABOUT BECOMING THE BEST OBSERVER OF YOURSELF YOU CAN.**

## SO HOW DO WE LIVE?

If that outcome is true for all of us, then something about the change framework is flexible and can apply to all of us. It does not mean we are all in the same box, right? It's a framework that we can uniquely customize for ourselves. Of course, we want to be happy. We all want to be at choice and have personal power, especially now.

We are at an important time in our human evolution. It is more critical now than ever to be at choice, because we cannot leave it up to those around us. We cannot suspend our power in the hopes another person will step up on our behalf, or that our political system will be miraculously overhauled. If we relinquish power to those systems and those systems do not move us forward the way we hope, our future looks pretty dismal. If each of us operates from a place of awareness and personal empowerment, I believe we can achieve great things together.

## LIVING IN DISSATISFACTION

If you picked up this book, you are probably experiencing some level of dissatisfaction with your journey. Having read the book, my wish is that you feel what I feel: hope. Have you become aware of something now that you did not know before? How will this new awareness impact future decisions?

Be curious and do not judge yourself. Be resolute that each step, no matter what direction, is a step closer to the goal at hand. Know that where there is learning, there is choice and power.

We need to rely on others. We are not on our own. We all need to work through perspective shifts, and we cannot do it by ourselves. For those raising children, you know it takes a lot more than one time for a lesson to stick. In fact, it requires repeating for longer than eighteen years. That is the way it works. Why wouldn't that be true for us in other areas of our lives?

Revisit this book, and know that you are learning what you need to learn when you need to learn it. Remember you are not alone. Who are your friends, your peers, and your resources? Do you have a coach, a therapist, or someone who helps you when you are stuck? Do you have a support system that helps you to re-remember and re-orient yourself?Let this book be a tool on your journey, one you can pick up again and again, when you find your hope waning. If you find yourself not being observant, look through and see which duality you might be avoiding. Each read, I hope, will bring you a new awareness, a new perspective shift of something you didn't see before. Pick up the mantle of your own personal journey, and commit to coming back and re-acquainting yourself with some of the principles here.

And always, always, commit to continue to learn.

# PIVOT EXERCISE

If you are feeling "stuck" and need to make a pivot, this book will help you get unstuck. Read the following questions, write down your answers using clear language.

## 1. ARE YOU CURIOUS ABOUT HOW YOU APPROACH CHANGE?

a. Are you aware there is a change framework?

b. Are you open to learning and experimenting with a change framework?

## 2. ARE YOU ABLE TO CLEARLY DEFINE THE CURRENT STATE AND DESIRED, FUTURE STATE OF CHANGE?

a. Are you able to clearly define the transition state; what lies between the current and future states?

## 3. ARE YOU APPROACHING THE CHANGE EVENT FROM A BALANCED RIGHT OR LEFT-BRAINED PERSPECTIVE?

## 4. ARE YOU FOCUSING ON BLAME OR THE HEART OF THE MATTER?

## 5. ARE YOU AWARE OF THE DECISION INTEGERS THAT ADD UP TO THE CREATE THE OUTCOME YOU DESIRE (I.E,. 1+1=2)?

## 6. HAVE YOU EVALUATED THE WHAT AND THE HOW OF THE CHANGE EVENT SEPARATELY?

## 7. HAVE YOU EVALUATED WHAT SUCCESS MEANS TO YOU, SEPARATELY FROM ANY GOAL OR CHANGE EVENT?

## 8. DID YOU INITIATE THE CHANGE OR WAS IT INITIATED BY OTHERS?

## 9. ARE YOU AWARE OF YOUR CHANGE AUDIENCE?

a. Who is impacted by this change and what is their perspective?

b. What might they need to come up to speed with the change?

## 10. WHAT IS THE "NEXT" STEP WITHIN THE CHANGE?

a. Are you trying to make the "right" next step or are you open to making any step in any direction?

b. What judgment might you hold about the next step or the outcome?

c. Are you open to the idea that progress is not linear?

d. Are you OK with making a "bad" choice?

## 11. WHAT ARE YOUR CORE VALUES?

a. Are you making decisions based on core values?

b. Have you created any shadow values?

c. How are your core values informing your decisions?

## 12. WHAT ARE YOUR BELIEFS?

a. How are your beliefs informing your decisions?

## 13. WHAT EMOTIONS MIGHT YOU FEEL ABOUT THE CHANGE?

a. How are your emotions informing your decisions?

John Spenker is a catalyst for change and the founder of Synergistic Coaching & Consulting, LLC where he specializes in change management for organizations, teams and individuals.

Change management is all about understanding our behavior and how our behavior affects our ability to achieve goals for ourselves and our organizations. Using Pivot Your Perspective-Your Change Journey he helps clients say yes to change and open doors to Possibility, Potential, and Purpose.

Visit John at www.spenker.com.

54405835R00078

Made in the USA
San Bernardino, CA
16 October 2017